GUNSLINGERS in Action

COVER PAINTING:
"SQUATTER SWATTER" AH-1G Cobra
flown by Capt. (then 1/Lt.) Hugh Mills,
Vietnam November, Dec. 1969. This was
one of 3 Snakes flown by Lt. Dean Siner,
who finished his tour in October 1969.
Mills left the aero scouts to fly this Cobra
the last two months of his tour.

by Lou Drendel

squadron/signal publications

PHOTO CREDITS:
U.S. Army
Hugh Mills
Lou Drendel
Dave Burton
Bill Gambriel
Bell Helicopter
Sikorsky
Capt. John Kelly

All Photos Official U.S. Army unless otherwise noted.

INTRODUCTION

When AIRCRAFT OF THE VIETNAM WAR was published, one of the critical reviews I received lamented the lack of coverage of Army Aviation. The reviewer correctly pointed out that the Army had far more aircraft in Vietnam than any other service, and on that basis they should receive a proportionate amount of space. That is logic that is hard to refute, and I will not try. I can only say that photos and information concerning Army Aviation have not been easy to come by, and were it not for the interest and efforts of one Army Aviator, this book would never have come to fruition.

The Vietnam War fostered significant tactical and technological advances in Army Aviation, and produced innumerable acts of courage and personal daring on the part of Army pilots. With that in mind, I decided early in the planning for the **"In Action"** series to do a book on Army Aviation, despite the possible difficulties.

Though the range of aircraft types operated by the Army in the Vietnam War was relatively narrow, the sheer numbers of aircraft made the choice of which one to concentrate on tough. A chance meeting with the Army Aviator who is the central character in the action portion of this book solved that problem, but created another one for me. In relating his experiences to me, he convinced me that I would have to modify the standard "In Action" series format. His personal narratives of the missions he flew were so exciting that I frankly doubted that I could stick to our "nuts and bolts" description of the subject aircraft. With that in mind, I have shifted the emphasis to a mission concept, and more importantly, to the people who made it work. That concept is the helicopter gunship, and the people who flew the gunships and scouts.

AB UNO DISCE OMNES

By now it must be apparent to the most insensitive of us that the Vietnam War was a severe strain upon the American psyche. The reasons for this national emotional upheaval run the gamut from the sheer length of the war, to the depth and detail in which it was covered by the media, which often seemed to disassociate itself from national interests in it's eagerness to champion the winning side. By any military standards, the communist Tet Offensive of 1968 was a defeat for the enemy. But in the eyes of the media, it considerably dimmed "the light at the end of the tunnel", and caused a drastic shift in the emphasis of reporting from the war zone. The news coverage took on a much more critical nature, and the U.S. Army was most open to criticism as a result of personnel problems caused by questionable civilian decisions made early in the conflict.

Perhaps the most abhorred decision (by military men) was the determination not to mobilize the Reserves or National Guard during the build-up phase, or in the ensuing years when the regular replacement of combat troops was made at fixed intervals, regardless of the tactical situation. The effect of this decision was to weaken the leadership and ranks of the Army in many vital areas. It should be pointed out that this was not a complete weakening, nor was the Army unable to cope with it in every case. But under the circumstances, which had begun to stress quantity at the expense of quality, it was almost inevitable that an incompetent officer should be placed in a position where he could commit an act which would cause grievous damage to the image of the Army, and mask the many acts of selfless courage and sacrifice made by countless other Army Officers. The story of that incident achieved widespread and sensational coverage. The sordid details shocked and sickened the American public into outraged disbelief. Could this be the same army that had made the world safe for democracy, that had achieved total victory over the most heinous totalitarian regimes in the history of mankind a mere twenty-five years previously? It was the same army, manned by the same kind of people for the most part. The difference was in the objectives of the war, or rather in the definition of those objectives. The enemy was no less evil, and the motivation of the best people in our army no less high-minded. But, while the cost of the war was very visible, the rewards for winning it were not. Did the Army feel abandoned and unduly criticised? Some may have. The best did not. They were professionals, with faith in themselves and their country. They did their jobs to the best of their abilities, many times making the ultimate sacrifice for the United States.

Centuries from now, some future society may uncover newspapers, magazines, videotapes, and radio transcriptions from America in the late 1960's. Based on this evidence, they might conclude that the Vietnam War generation was made up of a totally disaffected youth. They will see the drop-outs, deserters, and mistakes in uniform. They will see very little of the youth who, out of a sense of duty, fought gallantly in Vietnam. The latter, though clearly the majority, deserve better than they have received in the way of recognition for their contribution.

Captain Hugh Mills is an exceptional example of the forgotten plurality who fought the Vietnam War. Hugh Mills left Arkansas Tech after one semester to enlist in the Army on February 1, 1967. He entered the Army as a private and, after basic training, applied for and was accepted to Officer Candidate School. Upon graduation from OCS at Fort Knox, he was commissioned a 2nd Lt. of Armor in December of 1967. From Fort Knox he went to flight school, graduating in November, 1968. He arrived in Vietnam on New Years Day, 1969, and immediately assumed command of the Aero Scout Platoon of Troop D, 1st Squadron, Fourth Cavalry, of the 1st Infantry Division. Following a one year tour in Vietnam, he served for a year in Germany, and a year with the Army Recruiting Service in San Antonio. From there, he went through the Cobra Instructor Pilot Sylabus at Fort Hunter and returned to Vietnam, this time as a Cobra gunship pilot with the 101st Airborne Division. Four and a half months through this tour, the 101st "stood down", and left Vietnam. Hugh Mills returned to his old unit, in the South Vietnamese delta, and reassumed command of the Aero Scouts.

In two years of combat flying he collected 95 decorations, including three Silver Stars, five Distinguished Flying Crosses, three Bronze Stars with "V", sixty-six Air Medals, six Air Medals with "V", the Army Commendation Medal with "V", six Purple Hearts, the Vietnamese DFC, the Vietnamese Cross of Gallantry with Silver Star, the Vietnamese Medal of Honor, the Vietnam Service Medal, and the Vietnam Campaign Ribbon. He flew 3300 combat hours in 1019 combat missions. (75% of it in OH-6A scouts, the balance in Cobra Gunships.) He was shot down 16 times. Some of the highlights of those missions will be related to the reader as he related them to me.

Since Hugh Mills' exploits are related in his own words, it might be helpful to the reader to have a clearer picture of this modern day Army Aviator. As an author, one of his attributes which impressed me most was his almost total recall of dates, times, call signs, and other details pertinent to the incident he was describing. But that's getting ahead of myself in this word-picture.

Hugh Mills is a six-footer with a spare, rangy build. He has a firm handshake, gazes at the world through clear blue fighter pilot's eyes, and talks of his experiences with an unabashedly firm and positive voice. Though he likes to compare the Army Helicopter Pilot with the Army Air Corps fighter pilots of World War II, you would never associate him with some of the randy, reckless hot shots of that era. There is no braggadocio in his manner when he talks. Neither is there any false modesty. He admits to having become a very religious person as a result of his experiences in Vietnam. He is the kind of commander who will always lead the "tough ones". The kind of commander troops instinctively respect and follow.

The title of this brief dissertation is "AB UNO DISCE OMNES" which, translated from Latin means; "From one specimen judge all the rest". Earlier I alluded to a specimen which received what I felt was an inordinate amount of publicity for his deeds. This is my plea for equal time for those who come from a completely different mold. As long as there are people like Hugh Mills working their way up in the Army, we will have a good Army, an Army that we can be proud of, and that will always represent our best interests.

BIRTH OF THE GUNSHIP

As is often the case with an innovative invention, the offensive potential of the helicopter was largely overlooked during it's early operational employment. The vision and foresight of Army planners was stifled by several factors. The prototype **Sikorsky XR-4** was tested by the Army Material Center at Wright Field, but the inherent instability of the first helicopter was discouraging, and the immediacy of mid-1942 problems dictated development of more conventional aerial gun-platforms. The helicopter gunship was not completely forgotten during World War II, for the promise of tactical mobility and firepower kept testing programs alive.

It took the creation of the United States Air Force, and the emasculation of Army Aviation to halt development programs in the United States. The Air Force jealously guarded their newly won sovereignty, and it was not until 1950 that the Army and Bell collaborated on experimentally arming the **OH-13** helicopter. The first use of the armed helicopter in combat is variously credited to the U.S. Army in Korea, (an OH-13 with a bazooka) or to the French in Indochina. (Either an OH-13 with machine gunners riding the side-mounted litters, or H-21's with 20mm cannon, depending upon whose version you believe.) The French are also credited with employing a wide range of weaponry in a variety of helicopters during their abortive struggle to maintain their hold on Algeria. Several of these experiments, which were often the result of imaginative tamperings, provided the basis of later and more formal developmental work on the helicopter gunship. But without official sanction, or high-level impetus, the armed helicopter development program floundered in limbo. It took a visionary with enough faith, and enough rank, to put the program on it's feet.

Brigadier General Carl Hutton had the rank, the vision, and a healthy determination to get the Army back into the sky. The Army wasn't thinking of limited wars in 1956, but General Hutton envisioned a 100 percent armed mobile force for employment on the nuclear battlefield. He asked Colonel Jay D. Vanderpool to form the prototype unit.

Vanderpool's first efforts were directed at successfully arming the helicopter. He armed the **OH-13** with rockets and a 50 caliber machine gun. The experiments were surprisingly successful, in light of the discouraging reports on the 1940's attempts at arming the helicopter. Vanderpool was particularly anxious to perfect an anti-tank weapon for the helicopter. Though his experiments proved the feasibility of arming the helicopter, the helicopter tank killer was not to see consistent success until several years later.

Feeling that the problem of providing intrinsic tactical fire support for his "Sky Cavalry" was well on the way to being solved, Hutton next concentrated on establishing an airmobile tactical force of company size. He borrowed the Duke of Wellington's ideas on cavalry, in which the cavalrymen fought from mounts, the dragoons dismounted to fight as infantry, and all were supported by horsemobile artillery. The unit which was the forerunner of the airmobile divisions who fought in Vietnam was formed in March of 1957. It consisted of 11 officers, 16 enlisted men, and 10 helicopters, and was designated the aerial combat reconnaissance platoon provisional (experimental), or ACR. Once formed, the unit traveled from base to base, demonstrating and trying to sell the airmobile concept to Army commanders.

During 1957 "Vanderpool's Fools", as they were jocularly known, continued their experiments with the armed helicopter. Among the helicopters and weapons they tried were the **OH-13**, with 4 30 caliber machine guns and rockets, the **H-21** and

Bell 207 Sioux Scout **made it's first flight in 1963. It was the forerunner of the Huey Cobra, having the tandem seating arrangement for gunner and pilot. It employed the** TAT-101 gun turret, **with twin 30 caliber machine guns. Prototype was underpowered, and a production version was never built. (Bell)**

UH-19, with a variety of rockets and machine guns, and the **CH-34** with 5 inch artillery rockets. As the 50's waned, the testing and experimenting continued, eventually leading to the expansion of the ACR to a company sized unit. The work done by Hutton's unit also led to the formalizing of tactics for the armed helicopter. The first armed helicopter company was formed on Okinawa July 25, 1962. It deployed to Vietnam in October, and received it's baptism of fire within a week. The last few skeptics grudgingly admitted the possibilities of the armed helicopter, and Secretary of Defense McNamara called for increased Army mobility via the vertical lift principle.

In 1962 the Army Tactical Mobility Requirements Board, under LTG Hamilton Howze, commander of the Strategic Army Command and the 18th Airborne Corps, was convened in order to work out the organization of an air assault division. The recommendations of the Howze Board led to the rejuvenation of Army aviation, and helicopters replaced land vehicles as the prime movers of infantry units. Though the board stressed the need for an advanced design of armed helicopter to escort and provide covering fire for the troop carrying helicopters, Air Force insistence that tactical air support was their exclusive domain restricted the flow of development funds for the gunships. It remained for the arena of battle in the jungles of Vietnam to prove the need for the gunship.

H-34 firing Bullpup missile during tests.

Experiments with an armed version of the H-34 were conducted in 1956.

H-34's were also armed with Bullpup missiles and Hughes 20mm revolver cannon pod. (400 rounds)

Armed H-34 carried twin 20mm cannon, twin 50 caliber MG, 40 2.5 FFAR, twin 30 cal MG (window mounted), 4 30 cal. MG (tracer firing for rocket aiming), 2 5" Tiny Tim Rockets, and one 50 cal MG in window mount.

Additional H-34 details, including cockpit pantograph sight, and waist 50 cal. MG mount.

Armament mounting on side of H-34, including 2.5" FFAR tubes, .30 and .50 cal. MG's, and 20mm cannon.

Sikorsky SH-3 Sea King mounting 40 4.5" rocket tubes, capable of elevation and depression. (Sikorsky)

20mm cannon and 2.75 rocket pod.

Rear ramp mounted .50 cal. MG.

Window mounted .50 cal. MG.

In 1966 1st Air Cav Div evaluated 3 armed CH-47 Chinooks in combat. They mounted 40mm M-5 grenade launchers, 2.75 FFAR's, 20mm cannon, and five .50 cal. window mounted machine guns.

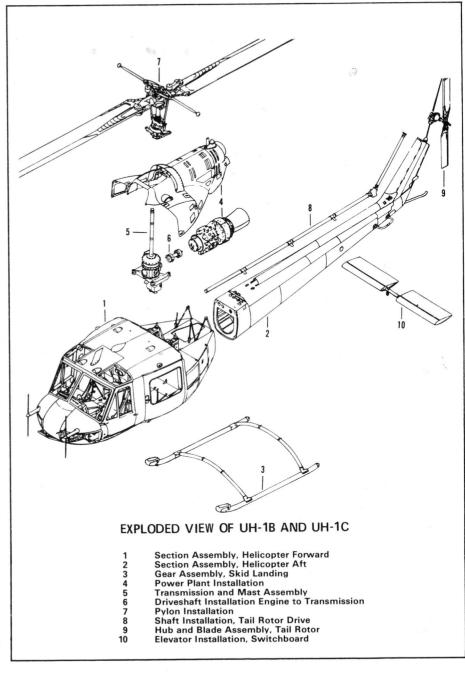

EXPLODED VIEW OF UH-1B AND UH-1C

1	Section Assembly, Helicopter Forward
2	Section Assembly, Helicopter Aft
3	Gear Assembly, Skid Landing
4	Power Plant Installation
5	Transmission and Mast Assembly
6	Driveshaft Installation Engine to Transmission
7	Pylon Installation
8	Shaft Installation, Tail Rotor Drive
9	Hub and Blade Assembly, Tail Rotor
10	Elevator Installation, Switchboard

The UH-1B was the first helicopter gunship to achieve widespread combat use. It was also the first to carry the name "Cobra". It is powered by the 1,100 shp T53-L-11 turbine engine, and could cruise at 85-95 mph. The model shown above was the most heavily armed version of the many variations the UH-1B/C was configured in. In addition to two door gunners with hand held M-60 machine guns, it was armed with the M-5 40mm grenade launcher (107 rounds), 2.75" rocket pods, and quad .30 cal. machine guns. Its success in escorting the troop carrying Hueys accelerated the development and production of the AH-1 Huey Cobra.

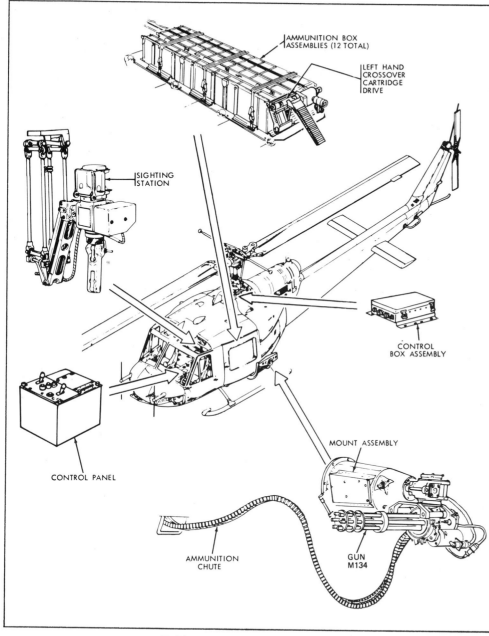

AMMUNITION BOX ASSEMBLIES (12 TOTAL)

LEFT HAND CROSSOVER CARTRIDGE DRIVE

SIGHTING STATION

CONTROL BOX ASSEMBLY

CONTROL PANEL

MOUNT ASSEMBLY

AMMUNITION CHUTE

GUN M134

M-21 SUBSYSTEM COMPONENTS

M-5 40mm grenade launcher, nose mounted on UH-1B.

XM-6 Quad mount, with 2.75" rockets and twin M-60's on an UH-1B at Tan Son Nhut, 1963.

10

Door gunner on UH-1B of 179th Avn Co "Playboys" Vietnam, 1965.

XM-156 mount, with M200A-1 rocket pod attached. Pod carries 19 rockets, which can be fired at the rate of 6 per second.

UH-1C flown by WO/1 Bill Gambriel, Vietnam 1969-70. (see color illustration in center section) When these pictures were taken it had just had windscreen and overhead greenhouse panels replaced, due to VC bullet damage. It was later destroyed in combat. (Bill Gambriel)

"Playboys" in action. (above and below) Lifting off for a mission in 1965, and firing rockets at VC in 1967.

UH-1B of 145th Avn Battalion, mounting XM31 20mm cannon is made ready for mission in 1966 (above), and prepares to begin firing run. (below) It was based at Bien Hoa.

Army UH-1B and Air Force A-1E Skyraider worked as "Hunter-Killer" Team in South Vietnam, 1964. Huey is armed with quad .30 cal MG and M157 rocket pods, and carries old gloss OD finish. "ARMY" on fuselage in white, yellow tail markings, white eagle on nose and fuselage.

UH-1D **of 25th Inf Div equipped with searchlight, night vision device and minigun for night support missions. (Dave Burton)**

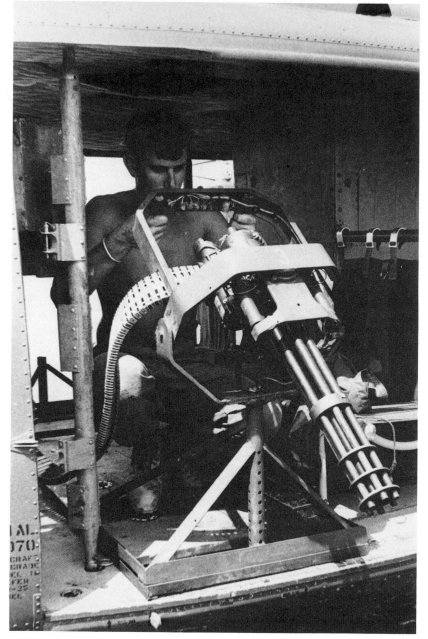

Details of Sagami mount for M-134 minigun **mounted on UH-1D of 25th Inf Div, at Chu Lai.**

UH-1D with quad .30 cal MG mount.

The prototype Huey Cobra as it looked during a promotional visit to Ft. Wolters in 1966. It has been retired and is on permanent display at the Patton Musuem, Ft. Knox, Ky.

Front cockpit of AH-1G Cobra. (Bell)

One of the first Cobra's to arrive in Vietnam. Note single minigun in turret, (TAT-102) and minigun pods on inboard stations. Dual landing lights were later replaced by single retractable unit under nose.

GUNSHIP TACTICS

Since the Air Cavalry is a relatively new addition to the Army, the tactics they used were often of the ad-lib variety. For the most part, they had no "book" to go by when they first went into action, and tactics were often evolved to meet prevailing conditions. Tactical policies might vary from unit to unit, but they generally followed a pattern. The pattern involved use of what came to be known as the **"Hunter-Killer Team"**. During his two tours of combat in Vietnam, Hugh Mills flew both the "hunter" and the "killer" phases of this mission. He explained the mission to me in these words:

"During 1969, I was assigned to Delta Troop, 1st Squadron, 4th Cavalry, 1st Infantry Division. The base camp for quarter-cav, which was the only air cavalry troop in the division, was Phu Loi, which is about fourteen miles north-northwest of Saigon. Our basic composition was the same as every other air cav troop, and consisted of a troop headquarters with a Major as Commanding Officer and a Captain as Executive Officer. Troop headquarters contained a maintenance section, mess and administration teams. The combat elements of the troop were as follows: 1st Platoon, which were the aero scouts. All call signs within the 1st platoon began with a one. For example, my call sign (as platoon commander) was "Darkhorse one-six" (The troop commander's call sign was

"Darkhorse six".) The second platoon composed the lift elements of the troop, and consisted of eight **UH-1D Hueys**. Lt. Wayne Macadoo was the commander of second platoon, and his call sign was "Darkhorse two-six". The third platoon was the Weapons, or Cobra platoon, with Captain Bill Church "Darkhorse three-six" in command. The fourth platoon was a rather unique unit. It was the infantry section of the air cav troop. It came to be known as the **"Aero Rifle Platoon"** or **"ARP's"**. These folks had various missions, and were transported to and from combat by the Huey platoon. Their commanding officer was Lt. Bob Harris whose call sign was "Darkhorse four-six".

In the early days of my first tour, we generally flew in what was commonly referred to as a "Pink Team". The coloring system of identifying the various units is peculiar to cavalry units. The white section, or "Whites", are the scouts. The red section is the gun platoon, and the blue section is the Aero Rifle Platoon. The common acronym used to describe infantry within the cavalry unit is "Blues", just as almost all other units describe infantry as "grunts". The hunter-killer team of Loach and Cobra came to be known as a "pink team" because of the coloring system. When the pink team found an enemy unit that they wanted to pin or pursue, they would call on the blues.

When the aero scout had picked out a landing zone, he marked it with a colored smoke grenade, got an idea of wind direction, obstacles in the LZ, and routes into and out of the landing zone. He would then make a complete sweep of the landing zone environs, to ensure that there were no enemy gun positions that could clobber the Hueys while they were most vulnerable, bringing the ARP's into the LZ. When all of this information had been collected, one of the Cobras would radio back to a forward base, where the Hueys were running up with the ARP's on board. At that time the Hueys would lift off.

While the Hueys were enroute, the aero scout would generally stay on top of the landing zone, low level, to ensure that no bad guys snuck into the area to zap the ARP's as they landed. While they were on the way, Darkhorse four-six had his own headset on, in the back of the lead Huey. The pilot of the Huey would put him up on the FM frequency that we used exclusively to communicate between the scouts and the ARP's, and I would give him a briefing. For example: Darkhorse four-six, this is Darkhorse one-six. Your landing zone will be a large, open rice paddy. You'll have trees on your left. You've got a water-filled dike on your right. You'll be coming into the landing zone on a heading of three two zero degrees, and you'll be cleared to suppress on both sides of the landing zone. The aircraft will be doing a one eighty in the LZ and going back out the way they came in, because you are going to have enemy activity at your twelve o'clock. You've got obstacles in the landing zone, in the form of scattered tree trunks. There is a little bit of ash on the ground, which may create a visibility problem when the aircraft come to a hover.

This information would be used by the Aero Rifle Platoon leader, who would use my approach axis to orient himself on the ground and on the map, so that when he got off the lead aircraft he wouldn't have to be fooling around with a compass and would automatically know which direction the enemy threat was. The information was also used by the pilot of the lead Huey, who was the flight leader. He would then go up on his VHF frequency and brief his pilots on the landing zone and the area in general, including such things as recent enemy activity or fire. Generally, we wouldn't put the ARP's into an area that was "hot". We would move the LZ a bit, to give them as sterile a situation to go into as possible. As the Hueys got into a position to observe, (usually when they spotted the Cobras orbiting at 1500 to 2,000 feet, they knew we were close-by) the flight lead would give me a call. I would give him a roger, and "smoke's out in the LZ!" At that time I would tell my crew chief which color to throw. When the flight lead spotted the smoke he would call me with a "roger, identify yellow, confirm yellow." (If it was yellow smoke.) We never told them which color we were going to throw, because the enemy was often on our frequencies and I have often had the designated color pop up all over the place when we confirmed a color before throwing it. That made it impossible to correctly identify the landing zone, and could lead to some serious complications in a hot situation. At the time the landing zone was marked, the scout would generally move out of the area. Some of the pilots liked to come up to altitude, some didn't. Generally, with the newer scout pilots, we liked to have them come up to altitude, where we were

Cobra **of the 334th Armed Helicopter Co, 12th Combat Aviation Gp, II Field Force, Vietnam, on a support mission, 1967.**

sure that they were out of the way. That saved the Cobras the trouble of dividing their attention between the scout, and the incoming Hueys. The Hueys would usually bring an extra pair of Snakes (Cobras) with them to assist in the "prep". The Cobra working with the Loach would retain his ordnance to protect the scout when the scout went back down to direct the activities of the ARP's. As the two Snakes who were accompanying the Hueys approached, they would also identify my smoke, and when the Hueys began their descent into the LZ, the lead Cobra would roll in on his initial pass. The Cobras would lay down suppressive fire with their rockets in a three sided box around the LZ, making repeated passes to cover the approach and exit of the Hueys. When the Hueys got down to their last 75 feet of approach, the flight lead would give his door gunners the O.K. to begin suppressive fire with their M-60 machine guns. While the door gunners were prepping, I usually stayed away from the area, because of the danger of ricochets. Once touch-down was complete, the door gunners would cease fire, the ARP's would dismount from both sides of the aircraft, and immediately establish a

Newly arrived Cobras await their baptism of fire in Vietnam.

Post-mission checklist is completed by Maj. Ronald Gray, CO of 1st Plt, 334th Armed Helicopter Co. "Playboys", at Bien Hoa, April, 1968. Note gloss black helmets, with bunny emblem on side. These were later replaced with the standard OD helmet.

Cobra with the XM-28 turret which replaced the TAT-102. It also mounts XM159 and M158 rocket pods. The 2.75 in. rockets come in 10 or 17 pound warhead variety, in HE, and in WP.

rudimentary defense perimeter. At that time, the Hueys would leave the LZ in the most expeditious manner. As soon as their escorting Cobras had them in tow, and they were well clear of the area, the "killer" Cobra overhead would go silent on UHF. We had three radios: UHF, VHF, and FM. The FM frequency was used to communicate with the ARP's, since they carried the PRC-25 radio. When the scout wanted to talk exclusively to the Cobra, he would use UHF. The policy in the troop was that when the scout was working low-level, he initiated all communications. Technique varied from pilot to pilot, but I liked to stay on FM, talking to the ARP's, describing what I saw, and what I was going to do next. The Cobra pilot would monitor these transmissions, and maintain a mental picture of the situation. I generally flew with Lt. Dean Siner, who was "Darkhorse three-one". We had been flying together long enough that Dean very seldom said anything to me at all, because when I worked low-level it bothered me to have to divide my attention from looking and talking. When scouting, if I talked to the people on the ground, or to my crew chief, I always keyed the mike rather than just use the intercom. That way, the Cobra pilot would pick up the same impressions that I did from what I saw, or felt in the area.

When the **Aero Rifle Platoon** was on the ground, and had established their perimeter, I would immediately go up on FM and get a communications check with the Aero Rifle Platoon leader's RTO. Once that communications link was established, I would come back over the ARP's, confirming that their position was secure. I would then move directly to the enemy threat that I wanted them to check out. If they were within visual range of the target I would drop a colored smoke grenade, generally red, to mark the enemy locations. After that I would move back to the LZ, and give them a heading to the target. For example: "Darkhorse four-six, this is Darkhorse one-six. Your target is an enemy bunker complex, two hundred meters to the north. Your heading from the LZ is zero one five degrees, and I'll let you know when you are within seventy-five meters of the first bunker I've spotted".

Once the ARP's had begun their advance, I would set up a circular pattern over the area, with the tip of the advance as one side of the circle, and the far side of the target as the other. That way, I could monitor activity within the target area, and keep the ARP's heading in the right direction. This relieved the ARP platoon leader of the burden of trying to read a compass as he advanced. I didn't fly with a map, as it is almost impossible to fly low-level, in a single pilot aircraft, and keep track of where you are on the map. All the mapwork was handled by the front seat pilot in the Cobra. The rearseater in the Cobra had to keep his eyes on me at all times, as the Loach is a small airplane anyway and when you're working down on top of the trees it is that much harder to see. The Cobra's job was to supply immediate suppressive fire if the Loach was fired upon, and that required knowing exactly where the scout was at all times.

When we first got our **Loaches,** they were OD overall, with no colorful markings on them at all, and that made them doubly hard to spot. Eventually we painted a solid white stripe down the top of the tail boom and on top of the "doghouse". This was a matter of pilot preference, and some of the pilots painted theirs with red, yellow, or international orange. After a while, individual taste came out. . .I painted a set of gold crossed sabres on the front of my aircraft, across the bubble. Each time the aircraft was hit, which was quite often in the scouts, the crew chief would paint a small purple heart next to the rear door. Each time the crew chief scored a kill, our policy was to paint a small black "coolie" hat with a skull and crossbones under it. As their skill increased with experience, many of them went over the 200 kill mark. We then began to designate ten kills with a silver hat and skull and crossbones.

When I left Vietnam after my first tour, I was flying **"Miss Clawd II"**. The first "Miss Clawd" had been shot down three or four times, but had been recovered and repaired each time, before finally sustaining irreparable damage. We had a string of silver coolie hats that ran the full side of the cockpit, and also 20 to 25 purple hearts painted on each side of the door.

The **OH-6A's** in our unit were armed with the XM27E1 minigun, set up to fire at a 2,000 or 4,000 rpm rate. (The pilot could control the rate of fire with his trigger switch.) The system was geared for

Cobras of the Cobra Transition School at Vung Tau, Vietnam. Note Cobra emblem on doghouse of Cobra below.

elevation and depression, but no traverse. (The pilot could get all the traverse he needed just by using the rudder pedals.) We didn't use the elevation or depression either, preferring to set the minigun up to fire straight ahead, then "walking" our tracers into the target with the flight controls. There was little need to use the elevation and depression anyway, since the average engagement range was about 25 meters. When you're firing at a 4,000 rounds-per-minute rate, at 25 meters, there is not much chance for a miss. . .even a lousy shot like me could get some pretty good hits. We carried 2,000 rounds of ammunition for the minigun.

In the back seat, the crew chief, who sat on the right rear of the aircraft was armed with an M-60 machine gun on a bungee cord. He carried a wooden ammo box at his feet with 3,000 rounds of M-60 ammunition. We flew with no doors on the aircraft at all, since they just obstructed vision, and made it harder to get out of a crashed airplane. We also strung a piece of wire across the bulkhead behind the pilot, to hang our smoke grenades on. We carried violet, green, white, yellow, and red high corrosive smoke grenades. Generally we carried 20 to 25. . .about 5 of each color. In an armored box to the left of the gunner's seat we carried our M-26 Frag grenades, white phosphorous grenades, concussion grenades, and CS grenades. The crew chief carried assorted armament in addition to this, depending on his personal preferences. We were standardized within the platoon on pistols. . .I didn't make a hard and fast rule on the type of pistol to be carried, as long as it was the same caliber for both pilot and crew chief. This was to ensure that in the event they were shot down, they could divide their ammunition according to the demands of the situation. My crew chief and I both carried the 45 automatic. Most crew chiefs would carry an M-79 grenade launcher, with assorted ammunition for it also. Some also carried M-16's or 12 gauge shotguns, as personal arms, in case we were shot down and had to defend ourselves on the ground. All scout pilots were issued the Colt CAR-15, which is a shortened version of the M-16 automatic rifle. With that, I carried three 30 round magazines taped together, plus a claymore bag with eight to ten more magazines. I carried my 45 automatic in a shoulder holster, with a round locked and loaded. I also had four or five spare magazines for the 45 in a belt pouch. As a backup weapon, I carried a S & W Model 10-5 .38 caliber snub nose on my belt. This was probably totally unnecessary, but it made me feel a little more secure. . .and besides, it looked good! A lot of the units in Vietnam used **"bombs"**. They would take a can of engine oil, for instance, and tape a thermite grenade to it. When they found an enemy bunker, they would drop this "bomb" on it in an attempt to burn it. Some of them also would tape four or five concussion grenades together, wrap belted M-60 ammunition around the grenades to form a bomb they called the **"daisy cutter"**. They would drop this on troops in the grass. I discouraged the use on this kind of conglomeration, primarily for safety reasons. Besides the inherent danger of jury-rigged explosives, I always preached a stand-off philosophy to my scout pilots. If you overfly the target you're just asking to get clobbered. We had the miniguns and the M-60 door gun for stand-off, and if we needed some explosive power, we had the Cobra overhead. And if you did get hit and go down, you were at least 25 to 30 meters away from the enemy troops. We had guys who overflew enemy positions, got hit, went down right in the middle of the bad guys. . .needless to say, we didn't get them out alive.

The Cobras, during this time period, (early in the Cobra's operational life) were using the old style armament. We had initially the **TAT 102** turret in the Cobra. That's the single **M-134 minigun.** The wing armament for the Snakes was of various types. They had two basic systems. The **"Heavy Hog"** carried four 159 pods, with 19 rockets each. The Heavy Hog was generally followed up by the light scout configuration on the Cobra. This included the XM-18E1 minigun pods, mounted inboard on each wing. Outboard they carried two 157 pods, with seven rockets each. We used three types of rockets at that time. We had the 17 pound warhead, the 10 pound warhead, and we had the fleschette rockets which contained 10,000 darts that sprayed in all directions when the rocket ignited. Personal armament for the Cobra pilots was about the same as that carried by scout pilots.

During 1969 we didn't have the sophisticated survival gear that the Air Force had. We didn't have the vests or the radios, which were a real premium item and awful tough to lay your hands on. My scouts were the only people in the division, other than the Aero Rifle Platoon, that were authorized to wear the camouflaged jungle suits. (We didn't have Nomex flight suits at that time.) We also didn't wear the standard issue camouflage suits, as they were in short supply and the ARP's needed all they could get their hands on. We ended up adopting the Korean tiger suit type of camouflage suit.

Working with the Aero Rifle Platoon was the mission we enjoyed the most, because you got to see more action and more results. You could guide the troops into an area that you wanted checked out more thoroughly. Maybe a bunker, or a fireplace, or some laundry hanging in the middle of the jungle. If they made contact, the scout would get right on top of the contact, in a right hand orbit around the target. (Both pilot and gunner sit on the right side of the Loach, so both had good visual contact in the right hand orbit.) The Cobra would cover the Loach, keeping an eye out for movement on the outside of the scout's orbit. Using this method, the scout could direct the fire of the ARP's, even though the ARP's often couldn't see the enemy threat. For instance: I would get a hold of the ARP platoon leader's RTO and tell him: "O.K., you've got two enemy soldiers in a bunker, five by five, twenty five meters to your front. Move over by the M-60 machine gun." He and the platoon leader would move to the M-60, and I would come up with: "O.K., move the barrel about 12 inches to the right, and fire a burst." They would fire, and by observing the tracers and the bullet strikes, I could further direct their movement of the machine gun barrel until we had hits on the enemy position. We could do the same thing with the M-79 grenade launchers and the M-16's. After working together many times, the ARP's got quite proficient at this indirect fire technique, and it proved successful for us.

One of the missions performed by the Aero Rifle Platoon was search and seizure. We would fly them into a road between two villages and they would set up a roadblock, checking traffic on the road. They had Vietnamese National Police to assist them on this mission, doing the interpreting and checking credentials of the people they stopped. Within the Aero Rifle Platoon we had four **"Kit Carson"** scouts. These were ex-Viet Cong or NVA that had rallied to the Government side, and had volunteered to go into combat against their former compatriots as scouts for American units. Overseeing the activities of the Kit Carsons in our unit was an NCO by the name of Sergeant Nguyen, who was born in North Vietnam, and had been teaching school in the South when the war broke out. In my opinion, the Kit Carsons were invaluable in the field, as they could read signs that the enemy left, and which we might miss. When the time came for a fella to go down into a bunker and roust out the enemy, it was usually the Kit Carsons who volunteered. On many occasions I saw these ex-VC run into the line of fire to pull a wounded American to safety, so there was no question of their loyalty. While I was there, we went through six or eight Kit Carsons. All were killed. All died in battle, fighting along side of Americans. I have nothing but the greatest of respect for the Kit Carson scouts who served with us.

Another vital mission performed by the ARP's was the security of downed aircraft anywhere in the division area. The ARP's weren't used every day for reconnaissance and ground patrol. Many days they had "Strip Alert" back at Phu Loi. If an aircraft was downed anywhere in the division area, the call would come back to troop headquarters, and we would scramble the ARP's to move out and secure the downed aircraft and extract the crew, if they had not already been rescued. They were always preceded by a hunter-killer team, which would sterilize the area before they moved in. The tactics used were much the same as I have described earlier, except that they would stay around the downed aircraft until "pipesmoke", the **CH-47 Chinook** came in to pick up the damaged aircraft.

The scouts didn't fly at night, except on a very few occasions, and then only under ideal weather conditions, and over flat terrain. The Loach is not an IFR equipped aircraft and does not handle well under instrument conditions. The curvature of the bubble creates a glare which makes visibility a sometime thing at night. Most of the night flying in the troop was done by the Cobra platoon.

Our missions were set up daily as follows: We would have two hunter-killer teams, consisting of a Cobra and Loach each, assigned to visual reconnaissance missions. These were known as VR-1 and VR-2. We would have

AH-1G's **of 1st Cav Div at Phuoc Vinh, RVN, 1969. Sharkmouth is black, teeth white, gums red, and outline black. It does not extend to underside of aircraft. Eyes are white, with light blue tips. (Capt. John Kelly)**

"Satan Snake". . .AH-1G Cobra flown by Lt. Dean Siner, who was the "Killer" on Hunter Killer missions with Hugh Mills. (Hugh Mills)

Hugh Mills' Cobra is reloaded with 17 lb. HEAT rockets between strikes.

two hunter-killer teams set up as Scramble teams. . .they were known as Scramble team one and Scramble team two. We would get our briefing at five in the morning, catch a quick cup of coffee, preflight the aircraft, and be off at first light with the two VR teams. They would move out to areas preselected by Division Headquarters, and perform their mission, taking as much time as was necessary to get the information. If they were fired upon, or got a contact of any kind, they would radio back to troop headquarters for additional assistance. When the call came in, the radio operator would turn on the amplifier, which broadcast throughout the troop area, and come up with a call such as: "Hunter-killer team on the hot spot! Scramble north!" At that time the crews of Scramble one would hit their aircraft at a dead run, crank, and be gone. The scout is the faster aircraft to crank, so he would normally be at a two foot hover in the revetment when the Cobra was still cranking. He would call the tower. . ."Phu Loi tower, this is Darkhorse one-six, hunter-killer team in the hot spot. We'll be scrambling north." At that time the tower would give him a "roger, break", and hold all traffic in the Phu Loi area until the team was off. As soon as the team had cleared the perimeter fence, low level high speed, the Cobra would call the scout with: "Darkhorse one six, this is three-six, my systems are hot." This would let the scout know that the Cobra had his armament systems on and was ready to deliver suppressive fire when called for. It would also remind the scout to check to see that his systems were hot, and that the crew chief had his M-60 loaded and ready for action. Then the Cobra would call flight operations for specific coordinates on the contact.

Once you got to an area, there was a ritual you followed. The Cobra would lead, with the scout flying formation on the left side of the Cobra. When you were in the area of the contact, and assuming there were not friendly troops on the ground to mark, the Cobra would identify the target by geographical reference. Then, since you had approached the area at altitude, (1500 feet) the scout would look for a spot to go down. The transition from altitude to low level is particularly dangerous, because that's when people are going to fire you up. . .you are vulnerable, because they can see you coming down, and they are most likely to take a chance and shoot at you. I would usually look for a large, open area, such as a field or rice paddy, and go down right in the middle of it.

When I decided where I wanted to go down, I would call the Cobra up and say: "O.K., thirty one, I'm going down in the large open paddy southwest of the target, and I'll be running in from southwest to northeast." Then I'd brief my gunner on the intercom. "O.K., Jim, we're going to be going down in the large open paddy to our three o'clock low. We'll be moving into the target on a northeast heading and we've got people in bunkers. I don't know their strength, or what kind of weapons they've got, but we can expect AK-47 and

CW3 Ken Evans of 334th Helicopter Co. "Playboys" dons helmet prior to taking off on a quick reaction strike in support of LRRP's of the 151st Rangers. (left) And enroute to target area "Red Catcher", Sept. 1969. (below)

possibly 50 caliber. If we do go down, you're escape and evasion will be to the southwest. . .make it all the way to the streambank and hold up. . .someone will pick you up. You'll be cleared to fire. . . there are no friendlies in the area, and use Darkhorse rules of engagement. . .no women and children. (And that's an up-and-up rule that we used. We didn't shoot women and children. We didn't shoot people unless they were clearly identified as enemy soldiers, armed and capable of doing a job on us. That was a policy, not my own, but a policy of mutual consent between all the pilots in the troop, and as far as I know, that was the policy of the great majority of all pilots in Vietnam. . .I never saw anyone violate that.) Once the crew chief was briefed, I would call the Cobra and we would recheck our weapons systems "hot". Then I would kick the aircraft over on it's right side with full right pedal, cyclic to the right, and collective all the way to the bottom. The aircraft would fall on it's right side, in a gentle right spiral straight down. About seventy-five feet off the ground, I would begin to pull left and aft on the cyclic, come on with the power, and eventually forward cyclic for airspeed. Utilizing this tactic, I would usually level off about five feet off the ground with forward airspeed. This made me a tough target for anyone on the ground who decided to take a shot at me on the way down. I was never hit coming out of altitude, using that tactic. Once we were down, and clear, the Cobra would begin to direct me to the target area, in the same manner as I worked with the ARP's. I tried to make my first pass through the target area at 60 to 65 knots, right on the trees. At that speed, you are past the target before they can get off a shot at you. During my initial reconnaissance of the area, I would move in erratic circles, keeping the speed up, until I had a pretty good idea of the disposition of the enemy troops. I would take a look at the trails in the area, checking to see what kind of traffic had been on them. An experienced scout can tell within a few hours how long it has been since the trails have been used, and how much traffic has been on them, and from that how many people he can expect to run up against. If the situation looked pretty hot, I would maintain my 65 knot speed. If it didn't look too hot, I would go into what I called my "tap dance". This was a technique I developed to make me a tougher target to hit. I would fly forward at about 40 knots, kicking left and right pedal alternately, and simultaneously "stir" the cyclic, just like a big tub of milk. This created a series of wild gyrations around both the horizontal and vertical axis of the airplane.

The crew chiefs would normally carry the M-60 machine gun in their right hand, and a red smoke grenade, with the pin pulled, in their left. They did this so that they could kick the grenade out the door the second we started taking fire. When that happened, I would turn my tail to the fire, and move smartly out of the area, calling: "One-six is taking fire!" The Cobra pilots knew that the red smoke marked the general area of the fire, and that my tail was pointing in

the direction from which it came. I would give them more specific instructions, such as: "Ten meters south of the smoke". They would roll on the target, and begin firing their rockets. About a second or two after leaving the immediate target area, I would give the Cobra a "one six is clear". This would let him know that I had safely exited the area, and that he could devote a majority of his time to hitting the target, and not worry about where I was. With the newer scout pilots, the Cobra pilot was forced to get him back up to altitude, make sure that he was straight, then put him in an orbit somewhere out of the way before hitting the target. Our experienced scouts would just take off out of the area, and hold clear, fifty to sixty meters away, down low, while the Cobras worked over the target. That saved a lot of time, and prevented the enemy getting too set for the Cobra attack.

That pretty well covered the job of the scout, whose mission was to find and fix the enemy location. . .not to engage. If a target was particularly hot, I would call in an Air Force FAC, and put down seven-fifties (750 lb. bombs) or napalm. I didn't take chances with fifty caliber machine guns, or high speed thirties, such as the SGM. When the enemy had those, I made sure there was a good chance that they had been neutralized before I went back in for an assessment. In the case of troops firing AK-47's or SKS, I would go back and have a look. Normally, after they were fired upon by the Cobra, they would go to ground, staying in the bunkers.

Hughs OH-6A "MISS CLAWD IV", flown by
Captain Hugh Mills, Veitnam 1972.

Lou Drendel
©1973

Rear cockpit pilot's seat.

AH-1G
Huey 'Cobra'

Front cockpit showing gunner's
position and turret sight. Red
buttons on top of handles fire
40mm grenade launcher. Trig-
gers at front of handles fire
the 7.62mm minigun.

UH-1C Gunship of the 129th Assault Helicopter Company, flown by
WO/1 Bill Gambriel, Veitnam 1969-70.

Rear cockpit, showing relative
positions of cyclic and collective pitch controls.

AH-1G
Huey 'Cobra'

Rear cockpit, showing pilot's
instrument panel and XM73
Reflex sight.

Loading minigun ammunition aboard a Cobra at Mai Loc, Vietnam, 1969. Also being loaded are the 2.75 rocket launchers. Max capacity for the minigun in the M-28A1 turret is 4,000 rounds, with 300 rounds for the 40mm grenade launcher. Minigun can be set to fire from 2,000 to 4,000 rounds per minute by the pilot while in flight. 40mm rate of fire is 450 RPM.

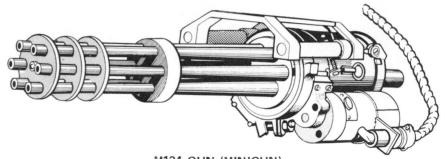

M134 GUN (MINIGUN)

ARP's of the 101st Airborne Division rearm the AH-1G Cobra of Capt. Hugh Mills at Quang Tri, while Mills discusses a point with co-pilot/gunner WO1 Dave Hartwick. Note the old M-1 Carbine carried in cockpit by Mills as personal armament. Six man crew of ARP's became quite proficient at rearming Cobras and engines were left turning during rearm to save time. December, 1971. (left)
Reloading M158A1 rocket pod on Cobra of Troop A, 7th Squadron, 17th Cav. Note dual miniguns. (below)

101st Cobras stir up the red dust of Khe Sahn as they take off for a mission against the NVA in northern South Vietnam, 1971.

Cobra on the flight line of 2nd Squadron 17th Avn Co, 101st Abn Div, Khe Sahn, 1971. Crummy weather was typical of that encountered in the highlands of South Vietnam.

Pilots refuel their Cobras at a forward refuel/rearm area during operations in support of 101st Airborne Troops at Fire Base Victory 12 miles south of the DMZ, 1969.

A LONG RESCUE MISSION. . .

From December, 1971, through February, 1972, the 101st Airborne was phasing down it's operations in I Corps, preparing to leave Vietnam. There were no ground combat units committed to action in northern South Vietnam. We were the only people up there involved in any combat. Our mission was to provide visual reconnaissance, security, and attack helicopter raids. We flew a standard **"Heavy Hunter-Killer Team"**, consisting of one **OH-6A** scout, two **AH-1G Cobras,** and a **UH-1H** with Rangers on board, to act as pickup aircraft in case someone went down.

On the particular day that this incident occured, I was giving check rides in the Cobra, fulfilling my obligations as the unit Instructor Pilot. We had a team out in the general area of Khe Sahn, performing a visual recce. The air mission commander was Captain Noel Harvey, who was flying the Huey.

They had finished their visual recon of "route red ball", which ran out to Khe Sahn from Camp Carroll, and were coming back to Quang Tri along highway QL-9. The two Cobras were leading the way, with the Loach in tow, and the Huey lagging a little behind. The whole force was at an approximate altitude of 6500 feet. As they passed Khe Sahn, the lead Cobra called the C & C aircraft to see if he was having any trouble keeping up. Captain Harvey keyed his mike, and began to assure the Cobra that he was doing O.K. They never heard all of his transmission. There was a loud noise over the radio and Captain Harvey called: "Taking fire, taking hits! . . . ." Then the radio went dead. Lt. Lew Brewer, who was leading the Cobras, immediately hauled his snake around. He spotted Harvey's Huey in flames at 5800 feet, going down. He repeatedly called Harvey on the radio, but got no answer. By the time they got to his position, Harvey was impacting on the ground. He landed about 700 yards due south of the old Marine base at Khe Sahn. The Cobras made an initial pass over the crashed Huey, and saw the crew get out on the ground. They called back to base, requesting additional help in the way of another fire team. The Loach, flown by WO/1 Major Hendricks, flew over the crash site and as he hovered to land, took a

WO/1 Bob Nowadnick shrugs into his survival vest on the dead run and he and pilot WO/1 Harry Zalessney answer a scramble call to provide support to LRRP's of the 151st Rangers. They were flying with 334th "Playboys", out of Long Binh, 1969.

heavy burst of AK-47 fire, which killed his door gunner and crippled his aircraft. He managed to limp off to Khe Sahn, where he landed and covered himself until another Huey came out to get him.

I got the word from Operations to scramble a fire team of Cobras. We had a bit of a hang-up initially, since we had no gunships "up" that were armed. The Snake that I was using was a trainer, but we quickly got squared away, and I led the team out. My wingman was CW/2 McDade Cockerall, "Charley Horse 45". "Old Mac" was the oldest officer in the troop and the only other IP in the unit. He was probably the finest gun pilot I have ever seen, bar none. Mac's aim was deadly, and he was cool and combat experienced. (Ex Airborne and Green Beret NCO). He was my mentor in gunships and transitioned my brain from 40 knots in scouts to 190 knots in gunships. He was an impressive figure with his full grey/black handlebar mustache, close cropped hair and ever present comment during rap sessions with new guys, "Hell, I invented that maneuver, son!"

While we were enroute to the crash site, the people on the ground began to take small arms fire on their position. The enemy was from 30 to 40 meters away from them and they could hear the NVA shouting back and forth to each other as they began to encircle the downed aircraft. They called Brewer for some supporting fire to discourage the enemy. Brewer immediately made some firing runs, putting in 2.75 rockets all around the downed Huey. This seemed to take the pressure off, as the NVA voices were stilled. I was on my way up the Ba Long Valley with the gunships, and still about 15 minutes out when they began to receive grenades on their position from 30 to 40 meters away. The Rangers began heaving grenades back at the still unseen enemy. One of the door gunners stood up and began firing his M-60. He was shot through the head and killed instantly. The enemy automatic weapons fire seemed to pick up in volume. Brewer had continued to make runs on the suspected enemy positions, but the close proximity of the NVA to the friendlies made his fire largely ineffective. The situation had deteriorated to a fire fight between the enemy force and the nine guys on the ground. Brewer called with an up-to-date appraisal of the situation while I was still seven minutes out. He was quite low on fuel, and had to break station to return to Quang Tri.

We pulled into the area at 1500 feet. I was acting as air mission commander and, since we had no other aircraft in the vicinity to guide us, I had to guess their general whereabouts by map coordinates. I spotted the downed aircraft and made one pass directly over the top of it at 50 feet. Captain Harvey waved as I went over, and pointed in the general direction of southwest. I pulled out, and still at 50 feet, made a wider sweep around the downed Huey.

About 200 meters out I looked down, and directly below me on route 616, which runs south out of Khe Sahn, I spotted 5 or 6 NVA dressed in dark green camouflage fatigues with pith helmets, carrying AK-47's. They looked up at me and ducked, but didn't fire. I radioed this information to Mac, and he rolled on them from 1500 feet. I swung out farther to the north, to see if there was any way that I could get the people on the ground to walk out to an improved highway about 150 meters away, where they could be picked up. As I did that, I flew over QL-9, which runs east and west, just south of Khe Sahn. Passing over the highway, I was fired on by an NVA 50 caliber machine gun, which missed me. I stayed low as I flew up to Khe Sahn, then popped up to 1500 feet to get some stand-off. I plotted the location of the 50 caliber, and we worked on it first, so that we could stay in the area. Mac got it. Captain Harvey called us on his PRC-25, and told us that they were not then getting a lot of fire, but that they could hear people moving around them. They estimated the enemy force at about company strength. After two passes at the 50 caliber site, we returned to the downed Huey. Since my Cobra was armed with the XM-135 20mm cannon Harvey requested that I come in and lace a pattern around their position. (The 20mm is much more accurate than the rockets we carried.) As I did this, Harvey reported that the AK-47 fire increased tremendously in intensity. The NVA were shouting commands back and forth again, and they made a frontal assault on the position of the crew. The Rangers beat back the charge, but in the fight the second Huey door gunner was killed. Harvey was hit in the arm, but continued to fight. Our estimate of enemy strength was now a company plus. . .completely surrounding the downed crew. . .and we had no way of getting them out.

My Troop Commander, Major Joe Seery, had arrived overhead in a **C & C Huey**, and I advised him of the situation. An Air Force Sidewinder FAC, flying an OA-2 also arrived on station and, after appraising the situation, called back to Danang, asking for a **Jolly Green** team from the 37th Aerospace Rescue and Recovery Squadron. The Jolly Greens were bounced immediately. They consisted of a pair of **A-1 "Sandies"**, a **C-130 King** aircraft, and two **HH-53 Jolly Greens.** The A-1's arrived on station first, while we were still working our rockets into the area around our people. Mac, who was flying a "Heavy Hog" expended all of his rockets, and I sent him back to rearm. At this time the whole troop had come up on "Scramble Alert" and they were arming all of our aircraft, and all of our Rangers to get in and get the crew out. The elapsed time since they had gone down was now about an hour and a half. Major Seery relayed the information back to the Commanding General of the 101st, General Hill, who "stood up" the 502nd Airborne Infantry Battalion, which had been in a "stand down" posture prior to leaving country. If it got too close to dark, and we still hadn't gotten them out, the 502nd was primed for an airmobile assault. We also had attached to us a company of CCN, known as the "Hoc Bao". They are a combination of Nung mercenaries and South Vietnamese Montagnards. Their missions include infiltration across the Laotian and North Vietnamese borders, where they set up ambushes along the Ho Chi Mihn Trail. They are vicious fighters. . .real good people to have on your side.

I returned to My Lac, a staging field between Khe Sahn and Quang Tri, reloaded and refueled and returned to the area. The two A-1's were on station. The flight lead was "Sandy Eight", his wingman "Sandy Seven". Since they had a capability to loiter longer, and deliver more ordnance, I relinquished control of the operation to Sandy Eight, who immediately established radio contact with Captain Harvey. Harvey, suffering from loss of blood, and severely shaken from the continuous enemy fire, told them that his people were about out of ammunition, and that they couldn't last much longer. The A-1's set up a race track pattern around the Huey and began to sterilize the area with 250 and 500 pound bombs, rockets, and 20mm cannon fire. After about 45 minutes of this, the enemy fire subsided. Sandy Eight decided to bring in the first Jolly Green. While all of this was going on, we flew a wider circle around the position, keeping an eye out for enemy movement on the roads. When we spotted them, we ran in with the turret miniguns, 40mm, and/or the 20mm M-35.

The first Jolly Green came to a hover over the downed crew, and put down a paramedic to aid the wounded. About the time his PJ touched the ground, the big HH-53 began to receive an intense volume of fire from the enemy. He was hit repeatedly, and was forced to abort, leaving the paramedic behind. He did manage to limp back to Danang, but was too badly damaged to fly again that day. The Sandies decided that the area was still too hot to bring in the second Jolly Green, so they went back to work on it, blasting away at the dense jungle around the Huey. They discussed with me the possibility of using an agent they called "Hobart". They told me that it was an incapacitating gas that would knock out everyone on the ground within 300 meters, good guys and bad. The after-effects would make them pretty sick for about a week, but that might be the only way they could cool the area down enough to get them out. . .and sick for a week was better than dead forever. I told them to do what they thought was necessary to accomplish the mission. They deferred their decision on Hobart for the time being and continued to work the area over with their conventional ordnance.

About that time, we spotted a platoon of NVA moving over a hillcrest, and down into a wooded draw. I rolled with my gunships,

"Pipesmoke" CH-47 **recovers a battle damaged Cobra after it was forced down in fighting around Can Tho, March 1968.**

"Blue Max" Cobra **escorts a "Nighthawk" Huey search ship in support of 1st Cav Div. Nighthawk carried 2 Xenon lights, 1 bank of C-130 landing lights, 1 starlight scope, (visible in picture) 1 minigun, and 1 50 cal MG.**

and let fly with 17 pound high explosive and fleschette rockets. We drew no return fire, and saw no further movement.

After about three hours of additional prep, the Sandies fired a protective smoke screen of white phosphorous, and called in the second Jolly Green, which was flown by the Squadron Commander. He came to a hover over the Huey, dropped his PJ, and began to extract the crew. The whole time he was at a hover, the Jolly Green put out a tremendous volume of fire from the miniguns in the sides and tail, and the A-1's provided a continuous blanket of 20mm fire around the area. They got all the people on the ground up, buttoned up, and headed for Danang without further incident. Every member of the downed drew, with the exception of 1/Lt. Neil Flynn, the co-pilot, was wounded. It was later determined that they had been under attack by a reinforced NVA battalion.

General Hill did insert the 502nd, which swept through the area, hoping to police up any remaining enemy. They counted 100 NVA bodies within 50 meters of the downed Huey, and we counted another 50 within 300 meters of the position. The Huey was too badly damaged to salvage, so after the infantry had retrieved the avionics and weapons, we blew it in place. The operation concluded with the extraction of the infantry at about 1830.

■ ■ ■

"Bad News" **(above), and** "Canned Heat" **(below) of the Blue Max 20th Aerial Rocket Artillery. (see rear cover profile for additional markings details.) (L. Wayne Richardson)**

"Palerider" **Markings details: upper half of mouth black, lower half red, white teeth, with red outline. White eyes, with black pupil and red outline. Name in white outline. (via Dan Wright)**

WO/1 Dan Wright with his Cobra "Pillow Power", so named because Wright's diminutive physical stature required the use of a pillow to enable him to see over the top of the panel. The pillow enhanced his effectiveness. (via Dan Wright)

Pilot of AH-1G refuels his Cobra at a forward refueling point, while he awaits the arrival of the C & C ship. Camau, Vietnam, 1971.

Wayne Richardson poses beside "Pandora's Box". (see profile on rear cover for complete markings.) (via Wayne Richardson)

Preliminary instruction in preflight of the AH-1G armed with 20mm Vulcan cannon, at Cobra Transition School, Vung Tau, Vietnam. Note: Installation of the XM-18 Pod on right inboard, and M-35 on left inboard is unusual.

334th Avn Co Cobra firing the M-35 20mm cannon at a target in Vietnam. Note spent shell casings below and behind Cobra.

SHOT DOWN. . .

The date was January 29, 1972. We were working a hunter-killer mission in the tri-border area. (The northwest corner of South Vietnam, where it meets the borders of Laos and North Vietnam.) "We" consisted of the standard hunter-killer team for that area and time, a pair of **AH-1G Cobras,** and an **OH-6A** scout, of Delta Troop, 3rd Squadron, 5th Cav, 101st Airborne Div. In addition to the hunter-killers, we also were accompanied by our own self-extraction team, which was a **UH-1N** loaded with Rangers. If one of the hunter-killers was shot down, the Huey could come in, lower the Rangers on rapelling ropes, (the Rangers were there strictly for perimeter defense while the rescue was being made) and extract the crew who had been shot down. We did this because we had no direct Jolly Green Giant support. The UH-1N was flown by Captain Joe Lasster, our Operations Officer. His call sign was Charley Horse three. I was air mission commander, and was flying a Cobra. My call sign was Charley Horse 38. My wingman was Lt. Lew Brewer, who was later shot down by a Strella missile, and killed at An Loc. His call sign was Charley Horse 34. The Loach was flown by WO/1 Tim Knight. SP/5 Rip Smith was his door gunner and their call sign was Charley Horse 11.

It was about four o'clock in the afternoon, and we had been conducting a visual reconnaissance along highway QL-9, from Khe Sahn to the Laotian border. It had been a relatively uneventful mission until I received a call from an Air Force "Covey" FAC, flying an **OV-10.** He had been putting in an air strike on some unfriendlies, and had just lost one of his F-4's to enemy ground fire. He wanted to know if we were in a position to give them some cover until the Jolly Greens arrived on the scene. I rogered that we could, and immediately headed for their area.

We arrived in the area and began to look for the downed F-4 crew. It was a heavily wooded area, with hills on either side of a small stream. The F-4 crew was somewhere in the base of the stream bed. Initially, we stayed high, at about 6,000 feet, hoping to catch sight of their parachutes in the trees. After a few passes, we decided to put the Loach down low. The FAC said that he had communications with the downed crew, (we couldn't talk to them because of a difference in frequencies) and he instructed them to let him know if and when they heard the Loach. If the Loach got close, he would let me know and I would direct the Loach onto their position. The Loach went down, and was down about seven or eight minutes, before he called up to me that he had spotted a base camp. The camp was active, had people in it that were running at the sight of him. I told him to disregard them, and to keep up a fast sweep to try to find the F-4 crew before we did anything else. About five minutes later, as the Loach was moving down the stream bed, he began to receive automatic weapons fire. He called "taking fire", and immediately broke right. As soon as he broke, we rolled from 6,000 feet with both gunships. I was lead and we made one pass with rockets, broke and climbed back up to about 1,500 feet. The Loach went back into the area, and again received small arms fire. As he broke, we rolled from 1,500 feet. As I fired my rockets this time, I experienced a double "hang fire" in the left outboard pod. The rocket motors fired, but the rockets stayed put long enough to tear off the aft end of the pod. It hit the tail rotor, knocking it off. The Cobra, unlike the Huey, won't fly straight and level without the tail rotor. (Because of the heavy weapons load in the nose, loss of center of gravity is uncontrollable.) The Cobra began to spin, nose low, to the right. I rolled the throttle off and held the cyclic centered, just to keep it level as it spun in. Just above the trees, I pulled the cyclic all the way to the stops. She stopped her spin and settled into the trees. The trees in that area were about 250 feet high, and upon first impact we lost the main rotor hub and rotor blades. We rolled inverted and plunged into the darkness below.

I guess I was unconscious for about five or six minutes. The aero scout hovered over the wreckage of our Cobra for about four minutes, and observing no life, decided to make a sweep of the immediate area. A few minutes later the Loach came back to find that I had gotten out of the wreck. I still hadn't regained my senses, because I don't remember doing what I did for the next few minutes. I crawled back into the Cobra, retrieved my survival gear and CAR-15 automatic rifle, which I had stowed behind the armoured seat, and discarded my helmet in favor of the Stetson cavalry hat we all wore when not flying. The Loach was hovering over us, and as I looked up at the door gunner, he pulled out a survival radio and started pointing to it, indicating that I should get mine out and start talking.

That clicked me back to my senses, and I started communicating. I told him that the co-pilot was badly injured, and that I had some kind of a head injury and felt that I could black out at any time, so please keep on talking to me. I walked back to the Cobra to check on my co-pilot, WO/1 John Bryant. The whole front of the Cobra was smashed and he had a broken back and neck. He was in a great deal of pain. The door gunner on the Loach told me that they should be able to get us out without too much trouble, and that the Huey was coming in to make the pickup.

The Huey came to a hover over us and dropped his rapelling ropes. They were about 40 feet short of hitting the ground, so he pulled up and moved it over about 75 to 100 meters to an area where the trees were not as tall or as thick. None of the Rangers had been in combat, and had never made a pickup under "real" conditions. One of the Rangers, the medic, had never rapelled out of a helicopter, and he forgot to double-loop the rope through his snaplink. He free-rapelled all the way to the ground, losing his M-16 in the top of a tree, and badly banging himself up enroute. Nevertheless, he was the first one to reach me, as the Rangers came thrashing through the jungle!

They moved in and helped me crawl back into the Cobra and drag the co-pilot out. We didn't know how we were going to get out, since the ropes were too short to reach us, the jungle was too thick to move very far in with an injured man, and there were no clearings within easy walking distance. Just then, one of the Rangers who had moved up the slope from our position began to fire his M-16 to cover himself as he backed down the hill towards us. The rest of the Rangers began to fan out upslope, setting up a defensive perimeter. Things were beginning to look increasingly grim for us. I called Brewer and explained the situation. I told him that they had better figure out some way to get us pretty quick, because the bad guys were probably converging on us, and I didn't think we could hold them off for very long. He told me that the Air Force FAC had called for a **Jolly Green Team,** which had been scrambled with a pair of **A-1 Skyraiders** for fire support.

The minutes dragged by, with everyone getting edgier by the second. There had been no additional contact with the enemy, but we all imagined them sneaking in on us, getting ready to lower the boom. I could hear the OV-10 overhead and occasionally spotted him as he made a pass over our position. After about a half an hour or so, there was a loud explosion about 25 meters downslope from us. I figured it was a grenade, and thought that the NVA were finally beginning to probe our position. I called the Cobra for some support. He replied that the explosion was a white phosphorous rocket from the OV-10, fired to mark our position. The Jolly Greens were in the area, and were coming in for the pickup.

A few minutes later the big **HH-53** came to a hover over us, blowing my hat off and down the stream bed. I never

Hugh Mills being hoisted aboard Jolly Green Giant rescue helicopter at the climax of the rescue operation. Wreckage of his Cobra is visible at top left of picture. (USAF)

recovered it. A door on the right side of the Jolly Green opened and a paramedic carrying a litter climbed on the jungle penetrator at the end of the hoist and began to make the 300 foot descent through the trees. When he reached the ground, we gently loaded Bryant into the litter, and they hauled him to safety. In deference to my head injury, they also made me ride the litter up to the Jolly Green. The rest of them came up two at a time on the jungle penetrator. When they had us all aboard and buttoned up, with the A-1's strafing on either side of us, we climbed for Danang and safety. The second Jolly Green in the team, with the aid of sophisticated tracking equipment, located the F-4 crew and made a successful pickup of them.

John Bryant spent three weeks at the 90th Evacuation Hospital in Danang, and then was medvac'ed to the States. He is in fairly good shape, though still under care at Brook Army Hospital. I would like to add that the Air Force was **good!** Very professional, and very cool under pressure. The HH-53 pilot was Captain Roger Colgrove, co-pilot was Major Jackson K. Scott, Jr., P.J.'s were Staff Sgt. Jimmie Minshaw, and Sgt. Harvey R. Pickelsimer. A1C William R. Pearson was the gunner. It was Colgrove's first pickup, and Pickelsimer's first time on the ground, and they did a fantastic job!

■ ■ ■

Various access panels are open in these shots for maintenance.

GUNNER'S INSTRUMENT PANEL

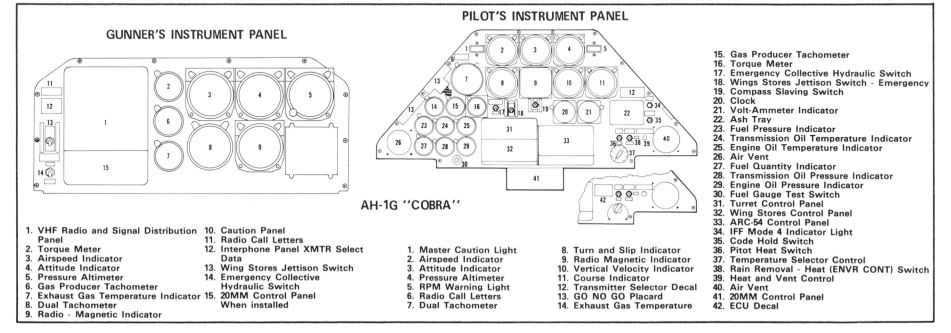

PILOT'S INSTRUMENT PANEL

AH-1G "COBRA"

1. VHF Radio and Signal Distribution Panel
2. Torque Meter
3. Airspeed Indicator
4. Attitude Indicator
5. Pressure Altimeter
6. Gas Producer Tachometer
7. Exhaust Gas Temperature Indicator
8. Dual Tachometer
9. Radio - Magnetic Indicator
10. Caution Panel
11. Radio Call Letters
12. Interphone Panel XMTR Select Data
13. Wing Stores Jettison Switch
14. Emergency Collective Hydraulic Switch
15. 20MM Control Panel When installed

1. Master Caution Light
2. Airspeed Indicator
3. Attitude Indicator
4. Pressure Altimeter
5. RPM Warning Light
6. Radio Call Letters
7. Dual Tachometer
8. Turn and Slip Indicator
9. Radio Magnetic Indicator
10. Vertical Velocity Indicator
11. Course Indicator
12. Transmitter Selector Decal
13. GO NO GO Placard
14. Exhaust Gas Temperature

15. Gas Producer Tachometer
16. Torque Meter
17. Emergency Collective Hydraulic Switch
18. Wings Stores Jettison Switch - Emergency
19. Compass Slaving Switch
20. Clock
21. Volt-Ammeter Indicator
22. Ash Tray
23. Fuel Pressure Indicator
24. Transmission Oil Temperature Indicator
25. Engine Oil Temperature Indicator
26. Air Vent
27. Fuel Quantity Indicator
28. Transmission Oil Pressure Indicator
29. Engine Oil Pressure Indicator
30. Fuel Gauge Test Switch
31. Turret Control Panel
32. Wing Stores Control Panel
33. ARC-54 Control Panel
34. IFF Mode 4 Indicator Light
35. Code Hold Switch
36. Pitot Heat Switch
37. Temperature Selector Control
38. Rain Removal - Heat (ENVR CONT) Switch
39. Heat and Vent Control
40. Air Vent
41. 20MM Control Panel
42. ECU Decal

Cobras of "F" Troop, 4th Cav Squadron, Hue-Phu Bai, Vietnam 1972, July/August. This unit took the brunt of the 1972 NVA invasion of South Vietnam and developed low-level tactics against enemy armor and missiles. They were the first unit to get the Strella Suppression kits for their Cobras. (shown installed in these photos) (see rear cover profile.) The Strella is a Soviet made heat seeking shoulder fired ground to air missile, which accounted for several shoot downs of U.S. aircraft during the invasion. (Ray Semora)

XM-35 20mm cannon mounted on Cobra.

Innards of XM-28E1 turret, showing details of the minigun.

M-158A1 seven shot, and M200A1 19 shot rocket launchers mounted on Cobra.

Rocket launchers from the front, showing suspension details.

Loach head-on. The OH-6A **first flew in 1963, and won a competitive evaluation trials over the Bell OH-4A, and Hiller OH-5A. It is powered by a 250 HP Allison T63 shaft-turbine. Rotor diameter is 26 ft., 4 in. Length 21 ft. 3 in. Max speed 161 mph. It is officially known as the "Cayuse". (Hugh Mills)**

AERO SCOUTS. . .

The tactics used by the Gunships, in conjunction with their scouts, have been outlined in preceding pages. In order to further explain how they worked Hugh Mills talked of several missions he flew as an aero scout.

The scout pilots are definitely the prima donnas of Army Aviation. They are generally young. (When I commanded the scout platoon in 1969, I was 21, and I was the oldest commissioned officer in the platoon. My second in command, 1Lt. Rod Willis, was 20, and all my pilots were 18 and 19 year old Warrent Officers. When I commanded the scout platoon again in 1972, I was 24 and considered an "old man" for a scout pilot.) Depending on his personality, what the scout pilot saw, and what he felt, was quite obvious to the Cobra pilot, just by the inflection of his voice. This is a big advantage, and was gained through the scheduling of the same crews together, day after day.

Being a scout pilot was one of the most dangerous and demanding jobs in the Army. During my 1969 tour, the squadron lost 32 men killed or wounded in action. The normal duty complement of pilots in the scout platoon was 15. Even though we sustained over 200% casualties, there were other units with a higher attrition rate.

One mission that stands out in my mind occured in mid-1969. My crew chief was SP/4 James E. Parker, and the Cobra pilot was Lt. Dean Siner. We were working along the Saigon River, west of the 1st Infantry Division's main base camp at Lai Khe, and east of the 25th Division's base camp at Cu Chi. The area we were working was along the western bank, and is known as "Loach Alley", because of the number of scouts that had been shot down there in the preceding year. There was a lot of enemy movement up and down the river, because it was a thoroughfare and one of their main supply routes. We were on a visual recon mission, about seven a.m., moving up the river in search of sampans. When we found a sampan, we would usually fire a couple of rounds through it, or drop a frag grenade on it, blowing it in place, then try to capture the occupants.

On that particular day we didn't find any sampans, but as we moved up the bank, I happened to look to my left and see some smoke coming up through the bamboo, about 35 meters from the river bank. I immediately called the Cobra, telling him that I thought I had a campfire. He came back with two clicks of his transmit button, indicating that he acknowledged my transmission, and that he also had the smoke in sight. We headed for the smoke on the tree tops, As we overflew the clearing, I made a hard right break and looked straight down at four VC soldiers whose breakfast we had interrupted. They obviously had not heard us coming, and began to scatter in panic as we roared over. (They had probably seen the Cobra, but since he was at altitude, didn't worry too much about him.) Parker opened up with the machine gun, and I hauled it around for another pass. On our second pass we dropped the red smoke, and turned outbound. Dean was already inbound on his firing run in the Cobra. His first rockets impacted the target when I was 15 meters from the target. That will give you an idea of the coordination we had achieved through practice. I had not said anything to him after my initial transmission, and yet he had determined what the target was, and had fired his rockets, confident that I would be clear of the target. As the smoke began to clear, I reversed and made another pass over the target area. We were not firing, and we received no fire on this pass. I turned and moved back into the area, slowing down to a hover over the target to get an assessment. Slowing through 40 knots, I spotted one body under the bamboo, pretty badly mangled and some equipment scattered around. Just then, right outside my right door, an AK-47 went off! (The sound of the AK-47 is unmistakable...it's a high ripping sound...a real bone-chiller!) In the same split second, the M-60 in the back seat erupted in answering fire. I put the nose down and hauled on the power, calling Siner to tell him that there was still some activity in the area. He came in for a second pass, putting about 40% of his ordance down. I moved in for a third time. On this pass we confirmed all four VC soldiers dead. There were some packs and weapons lying around, but they had been pretty badly chewed up by the Cobra.

When I was sure that there were no other VC around, I moved back towards the river, intending to continue the mission. About that time, Jim Parker hit his intercom floor button with his foot, and said; "Sir, if we took care of all the bad guys, could you take me to a hospital?" Since I hadn't heard any rounds hit the aircraft, I hadn't thought to take a look at Parker. I turned around to see him slumped in the gunner's seat, his neck and shoulders a mass of blood. He still had his M-60 in his right hand, and was clutching his neck with his left. There was a constant gush of arterial blood through his fingers. I quickly told the Cobra that Parker was hit, and that I was going to the 1st Infantry Division Surgical Hospital at Lai Khe. Siner called the hospital and forwarned them that I was inbound. I changed frequencies to the "Surgical Push", called them and told them that I would be inbound from the west in about three minutes with what appeared to be a neck shot, gushing arterial blood.

As I cleared the south perimeter, I saw the ambulance parked on the pad. Before I had shut down the engine, two medics had Parker loaded on a stretcher and were moving him inside. I climbed out of the airplane and began to inspect it for hits. There were no hits in the aircraft, but Jim's chickenplate (the body armor worn by helicopter crews), which was lying on the ground next to the pad had been hit by two AK-47 rounds. One of the rounds had hit it dead center, the other close to the neck line. It was the latter that had done the damage, deflecting through his neck, narrowly missing his

One of Hugh Mills' early Loaches, which he flew in 1969. Most Loaches in Vietnam were flown with the doors removed. This facilitated getting out in case of crash, and aided visibility. (Hugh Mills)

Another of Mills' mounts. (See cover painting for Darkhorse markings colors.) Loaches carried 2,000 rounds for minigun, which could be set to fire at 2,000 or 4,000 rounds per minute. (Hugh Mills)

Hugh Mills (left) with Rod Willis as he turned over command of the Aero Scout Platoon to Willis at the end of his first tour. (Hugh Mills)

Hugh Mills receives one of his many decorations from the Commanding General of the 1st Infantry Division, MG A.E. Milloy.

jugular, and going out the back of his neck, just below his skull. He was awfully lucky, since the round was armor piercing and had made a clean wound, doing no damage on its way through.

But that's the kind of guy Jim Parker was. He didn't say a word until the action was over. In fact, even though seriously wounded, he continued to fire his M-60 without letup, covering us until the Cobra could move back in. For this action, he received the Silver Star, as well as his seventh or eighth cluster to the Purple Heart.

Perhaps the most tenuous position I was ever in came about as a result of us getting shot down. It was July of 1969, and we were tracking a group of enemy soldiers that had ambushed a convoy on Route 13 the day before. They had left the area of the ambush during the night, and had taken no pains to cover their tracks as they fled to the west. We were at low level, and I was having such an easy time following their escape route that I committed a cardinal error in my pursuit of them. I moved my airspeed up as I became more and more anxious to overtake them. As a consequence, my observation suffered. After about ten minutes of chase, I spotted what appeared to be a 50 caliber machine gun pit off to my left. This was no surprise, as the Viet Cong soon learned that troops and/or aircraft would follow them after an ambush, and they often prepared anti-aircraft positions along their route of withdrawal. As I made a quick circle over the position, I noted that it was empty, and that the camouflage around it was at least 24 hours old, as it had started to turn brown. I was too intent on the empty pit, and failed to see a second, live, pit. As I completed my circle, I spotted the second pit just as we overflew it. It was manned with gun and crew, and before I could react, they fired a burst from a range of about 15 feet directly below us, which riddled the tail boom and one rotor blade. The aircraft immediately picked up a heavy vibration, the engine died, and we glided into the trees. (Once again, Parker was lucky, as a round came up through the floor right between his feet, missed him completely, and went out through the top of his "greenhouse".) As we settled into the trees, we rolled over on our right side, and I was pinned in the wreckage. I had hit my head on something as we went in, and I was in shock. Parker clambered out the left side of the aircraft, ran around to the front, kicked in the bubble, and helped me to struggle free. I grabbed my CAR-15, and a bandoleer of ammunition. We were about 15 meters from a large clearing, so we decided to get to it, figuring that our Cobras would be able to see us and provide covering fire. The clearing was about 150 meters across, and was covered with four foot elephant grass, which had overgrown the rice paddies. Interspersed throughout the clearing were rice dikes, which rose about two feet above the water level. It looked like an ideal spot to gain some cover and concealment. We ran about the first 15 feet into the paddy, then went down on all fours and began to crawl towards the center of the clearing. The Cobra overhead spotted us, and began his rocket run on the enemy positions on the other side of our downed Loach. We kept on going until we reached one of the rice dikes. It looked like a position we could defend, so we stopped to take stock of our situation. We had two 45 automatics, my snub nose 38, the CAR-15, M-60, and two fragmentation grenades that I carried on my belt. We sat still and watched the Cobra work. After about 15 minutes we began to hear voices in the jungle. There were shouted commands in Vietnamese, and we were sure that the enemy was looking for us. A few more minutes went by, and we could hear them moving closer to the clearing. Then I spotted two VC move to the edge of the jungle, look out into the clearing, and move back into the jungle. Ten more minutes went by, and suddenly we spotted six VC at the edge of the clearing! They formed on line, and began to fire into the clearing with AK-47s. They were firing at random, so we figured they didn't know where we were. We kept low and didn't return the fire. We knew that couldn't last, and it didn't. They finally spotted our trail, and began to fire into our area. Then there was a pause in their firing, and I jumped up and fired a burst from my CAR-15. We were about 75 feet away, but it was a good shot, catching the middle of the group. Two of them dropped, and the rest retreated into the jungle. The Cobra had seen me fire, and rolled in on the treeline. He got off four rockets and broke, covering himself with his minigun. They knew exactly where we were though, and we began to get rifle and machine gun fire on our position. The rice dike prevented us from getting hit, and we returned their fire when we could. The Cobra overhead was apparently out of rockets, but he kept making runs on the treeline with his minigun. About fifteen minutes went by, and we were getting low on ammunition. I decided that we would have to ditch the M-60 and try to move farther away from the enemy. It was only a matter of time before the Cobra ran out of minigun ammo, and we were going to be expended shortly. The VC would be able to stroll in and take us if we didn't get out. I was just about to give Parker the word, when we looked up and saw a flight of six Cobras, which had arrived on cue, just like the cavalry should. They didn't even circle. My Cobra directed them in, and they rolled, one after the other, and expended on the treeline. Parker and I jumped to our feet, completely forgetting the enemy fire, and cheered them on.

The Cobras either killed or completely intimidated the enemy, because the Troop Commander circled the clearing once in his UH-1H, then came to a hover over us without drawing a shot. They pulled us on board, ending one of the longest hours of my life.

One of my hairiest missions also turned out to be my last mission in Vietnam. I was scout team leader for a normal VR mission on 15 June, 1972. The gun team leader was Captain Chuck Chadborne, our gun platoon leader. His wingman was Captain Rick Rowland, a second tour veteran who had flown with Darkhorse in 1969 also.

We flew into what I could only characterize as an ambush. A group of people had seen us coming and had set up a machine gun. As I crossed a large open area, and headed for a woodline, I received an intense volume of fire from the woodline. The entire canopy of the Loach disintegrated, and that's the best way to describe it...plexiglass flew everywhere. I was hit in the right leg, and the force of the hit knocked my leg to the side, out the right door. My first instinct was to call; "Taking fire, taking hits, I'm hit! I'm going down!" My instrument panel was shattered, completely useless. It was without a doubt the worst hit that I had ever taken in an aircraft, regardless of whether or not I went down. The aircraft literally shuddered from the force of the hits, and it sounded like a swarm of angry bees in the cockpit. The rounds were everywhere!

The Cobras hit the source of the fire immediately, while I set the Loach down in a clearing about 200 meters away. I got out and took a look. The whole front of the aircraft was chewed up.. the shark's mouth we had painted on looked like a mouthful of cavities, there were so many holes in the front of the airplane. The round that hit me had gone through the right pedal, traveled between the sole of my boot and the heel, knocking the heel right off and my foot out the door.

Amazingly, though all the radios and instruments were shot out, the aircraft was still flyable, so we flew it back to Can Tho.

I didn't know it at the time, but that was to be my last combat mission. Two days later I got orders to the Armored Career Course, at Fort Knox. I went down to the repair shop, and with the help of my crew chief, painted out the name **"Miss Clawd"**, retiring it from combat. The aircraft, number 340, was returned to the scout platoon.

The name "Miss Clawd" originated in 1969, with my first Loach, and was named for a girl I had dated back in Arkansas, Miss Claudia Cox, of Hot Springs, Arkansas. The name survived through four aircraft that I flew.

■ ■ ■

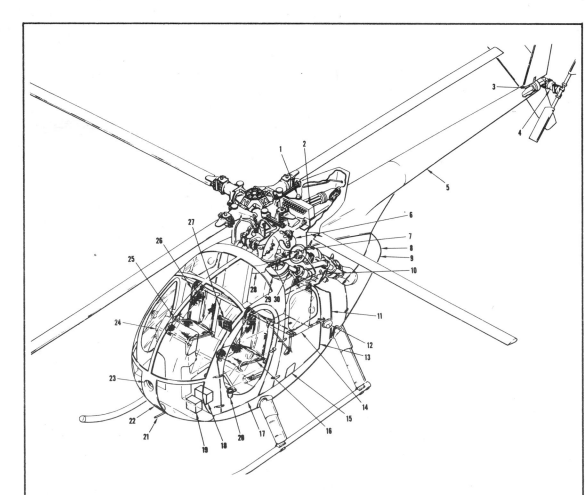

OH-6A GENERAL ARRANGEMENT DIAGRAM

1. Upper anticollision light
2. Engine air filter (Series 3 acft)
3. Tail rotor drive shaft
4. Tail rotor transmission
5. Tail boom
6. Engine oil tank
7. Oil cooler
8. Engine exhaust tail pipes
9. LH engine access door (right side typical)
10. Engine
11. Firewall
12. LH navigation light
13. LH cargo compartment door
14. Left passenger troop seat (right side typical)
15. Armament access door
16. Copilot's seat
17. LH pilot's compartment door
18. Radio and navigation equipment
19. Battery
20. Lower anticollision light
21. Pitot tube
22. Landing/hover light
23. External air inlet
24. Instrument panel and console
25. External power receptacle
26. Pilot's seat
27. Map case (checklist)
28. Main rotor transmission
29. Oil cooler blower
30. Main drive shaft

Scout at work. Door gunner peers intently into the jungle below, as Loach sweeps slowly over the treetops looking for enemy activity near Pleiku, 1969.

Scout leading ARP's to a suspected VC bunker complex, during operations near Pleiku in 1969. Units are from 7th Squadron, 17th Cav.

Loading a minigun of Loach belonging to 101st Airborne. Mai Lac RVN. White strips on bubble near door are antenna. Note position of pilot's M-16.

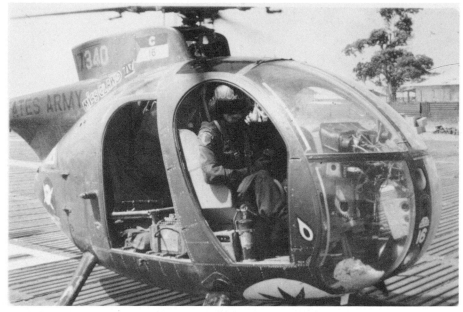

Hugh Mills in "Miss Clawd IV." External power receptacle is immediately behind fire extinguisher. Note position of "Darkhorse" emblem on front of Loach.

Loach hovering. Diminutive size of the OH-6A is evident. (Note that door gunner is not all the way in the aircraft!)

Mills and company with captured enemy flag and weapons, including AK-47 rifle and RPG-2.

TRIBUTE TO A FRIEND. . .

Rod Willis was my roommate in 1969, and second in command (Darkhorse 17). He took over the scouts when I left Vietnam. When I decided to return to Vietnam for a second tour, I called Rod in Savannah, where he was doing a stint as pilot training commander for South Vietnamese pilot-trainees. He decided to return to Nam with me. He was in the Delta the whole time and is a vital part of my story. He was my constant companion on almost all of my missions and, during times when I was refueling or rearming, or just taking a day off, Rod took over command of the scouts. His decorations mirror mine almost completely. Our techniques differed a bit, but not much. His door gunner was SP/5 Ken Stormer, a carbon copy of Jim Parker, and just as good! Rod learned quickly and was a natural scout. He had thick black hair and an almost boyish grin and manner. He was a real ladies man and charmed bar girls, teachers, nurses, and service girls all over Vietnam. Rod flew a Loach named **"Electric Olive II"**, which was painted identically to my "Miss Clawd". He was never without a big Colt 38 caliber revolver, which he wore in a low-hanging western holster. He doubled as air mission commander in the Delta, flying the command Huey. Because of his training experience, he worked well with the Vietnamese. During our tours together he personally risked his life, on four occasions that I can remember, to pick me up.....once when enemy troops were closing on my location.

In 1969, on an all-day mission to extract a pinned down U.S. force, Rod's quick wit and courage saved the day. He hovered over the pinned down force and fired his minigun in a 360 degree arc until tanks could extract the force. Not too exciting?...Except that he was shot down three times that day. Each time he was picked up, he would get another scout and return to the guys on the ground. He rightly deserved the Silver Star that he got for that action.

On another occasion, Rod was refueling at Muc Hoa between missions in 1972. A Loach that had been badly shot up was attempting a forced landing at the strip. The OH-6 lost its tail rotor and spun in the last 50 feet, bursting into flames upon impact. Rod, in full gear, sprinted 100 yards to the burning ship and helped the crew chief out. The CC said; "The pilot's still in there!" Without hesitating, Rod waded into the flames where WO/1 Tim Kolberg was tangled in the wreck, which was engulfed in burning jet fuel and exploding ammo. The blades were still turning as Rod ducked under them to free the struggling pilot. Rod freed Kolberg, pushed him to safety, and checked for others in the wreck before clearing out himself. As he ran from the wreck, a rotor blade dipped, hitting him in the back and knocking him 50 feet! He was wearing a back armor plate, or he would have been killed. He was hospitalized in Guam for three weeks, but refused return to the States in favor of more combat in Vietnam.

Rod and I often talked about the psychological aspects of combat flying, and I believe our views on it bear disclosure. Many pilots remark about being "psyched up" for a mission, or getting keyed up for combat. Rod and I had our own method, and it apparently worked, for it got us through a combined total of 5500 hours in four years of combat flying. We like to be keyed up on the ground, but not in the air. I tried to relax and smoke a cigarette before I cranked. We tried to maintain a very calm, relaxed state while scouting. We saw more and when needed, the boost of adrenalin that fear injects in a tight spot speeded up our reactions. The only drug that either of us ever used was natural adrenalin. Flying was our business, and it was really more of a day-to-day routine type of existence than it was an adventure. We took each day as calmly as possible, tried to control our fears, (a wise man never tries to conquer fear) and reacted to the situation at hand.

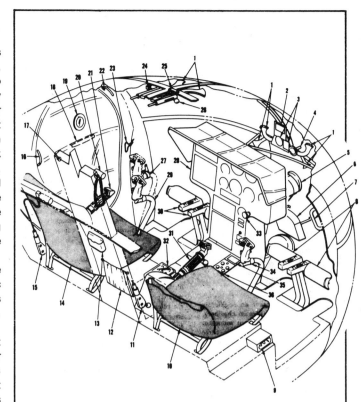

OH-6A FLIGHT COMPARTMENT

1. Cabin heat and defogging outlets
2. Pilot's Vne card
3. Compass and compass card
4. Outside air temperature thermometer
5. Fresh air inlet
6. Logbook holder
7. Assist handle (both pilot door frames)
8. Pilot's antitorque pedals
9. External power receptacle
10. Pilot's seat
11. Pilot's shoulder harness reel release lever
12. Map case
13. Ashtray
14. Copilot's seat
15. Copilot's shoulder harness reel release lever
16. Inside door handle (both doors, acft without armor provisions)
17. Utility light alternate location
18. Door pull (both doors; acft with armor provisions)
19. Door air vent (both doors)
20. Utility light
21. Copilot's collective stick
22. Inside door handle (both doors; acft with armor provisions)
23. Door jettison handle (both doors)
24. ENGINE DE-ICE control lever
25. BYPASS AIR CONTROL release handle
26. CABIN HEAT & DEFOG control lever
27. Copilot's cyclic stick stowage
28. Instrument panel
29. Copilot's cyclic stick (detachable)
30. Copilot's antitorque pedals
31. Pilot's collective stick
32. Circuit breaker panel
33. Fresh air inlet control knob
34. Pilot's cyclic stick
35. Ashtray
36. Electric Control console

Rangers practice dismounting from hovering Huey via rope ladder. Note rapelling rope also. (top right) ARP's aboard Darkhorse Huey prepare to lift off on a quick reaction scramble mission. Note armor around pilot's seat. (top left) ARP M-60 machine gun team in action. Note camouflage suits, which were not standard issue for infantry units in Vietnam. (left)

Hugh Mills in ARP mufti. Note dents made in his "Chickenplate" armor by AK-47 rounds. Body armour was a must item and saved many lives.

Remains of one of Hugh Mills' Loaches, after it was shot down and recovered. (Hugh Mills)

Blood splattered cockpit of Mills' Loach. Mills managed to force land the bullet riddled Loach, and returned to combat after convalescence. (Hugh Mills)

Mills and members of his troop examine the enemy machine gun that shot him down. (ARP's were inserted, pursued and killed enemy force, capturing many of their weapons.) (Hugh Mills)

Hugh Mills with Rod Willis (left) as he turned over command of the Aero Scouts at the end of his second combat tour. "Miss Clawd IV" was retired shortly after this photo was taken.